ROCKS AND MINERALS: 2ND GRADE SCIENCE WORKBOOK SERIES

SPEEDY
PUBLISHING

Speedy Publishing LLC
40 E. Main St. #1156
Newark, DE 19711
www.speedypublishing.com

Rock is a naturally
occurring solid aggregate
of one or more minerals
or mineraloids.

There are three different types of rocks based on the way they form, igneous, sedimentary and metamorphic.

NAME THAT ROCK!

FUN FACTS: An igneous rock. It is material for kitchen countertops and many other applications within the home.

G R N E

FUN FACTS: A rock formed from the rapid cooling of basaltic lava exposed at or very near the surface of a planet.

B   S   T

FUN FACTS: It is used for ornamental
purposes and as a gemstone.

B S D I N

FUN FACTS: It is widely used to make lightweight concrete or insulative low-density cinder blocks.

P   M   I   E

FUN FACTS: It was used as a structural stone by the
Inca and Mayan civilizations of South America.

D O   T E

FUN FACTS: A sedimentary rock composed largely of the minerals calcite and aragonite.

L   M   S   O   E

FUN FACTS: A sedimentary rock composed mainly
of sand-sized minerals or rock grains.

S _ N _ S T _ N _

FUN FACTS: A metamorphic rock. It is is commonly used for sculpture and as a building material.

M _ _ B _ E

FUN FACTS: A type of sandstone that contains quartz.

Q   A   R   Z   E

FUN FACTS: A metamorphic rock that
contains flakes of mica.

S   H   S   T

A mineral is an element or chemical compound that is normally crystalline and that has been formed as a result of geological processes. There are over 4000 different types of minerals.

NAME THAT MINERAL!

FUN FACTS: It is the most abundant metal found naturally on Earth.

A L M N M

FUN FACTS: Its pigment is most widely known
for use in jewelry, glass, and paint.

C   B   T

FUN FACTS: It is an essential nutrient to all living organisms.

C   P   R

FUN FACTS: It is the hardest natural material known and is often used for industrial cutting and polishing tools.

D _ _ M O _ D

FUN FACTS: A good conductor of electricity and heat.
It is the most popular precious metal for investments.

G   L

FUN FACTS: It is used to make bullets and is also used in radiation shields around X-ray equipment.

L _ _ D

FUN FACTS: It is the world's main source of aluminium.

B   U   X   T

S P H L R T

FUN FACTS: A magnetic rock. It is the
most magnetic mineral on earth.

M _ _ N _ T _ T E

FUN FACTS: A soft, shiny metal that is a good conductor of electricity.

S   _   _   V   _   R

FUN FACTS: The second most commonly found mineral on Earth.

Q _ _ R _ Z

FUN FACTS: Is found near hot springs/pools and volcanic areas, most notably in countries around the Pacific Ring of Fire.

S   L   F

ANSWER

GRANITE	LIMESTONE
BASALT	SANDSTONE
OBSIDIAN	MARBLE
PUMICE	QUARTZITE
DIORITE	SCHIST

ANSWER

ALUMINUM	BAUXITE
COBALT	SPHALERITE
COPPER	MAGNETITE
DIAMOND	SILVER
GOLD	QUARTZ
LEAD	SULFUR

www.ingramcontent.com/pod-product-compliance
Lightning Source LLC
Chambersburg PA
CBHW080946130726
48003CB00010BA/3114